Williamsburg—Three Hundred Years

Williamsburg— Three Hundred Years
Freedom's Journey

Photography by David M. Doody

Additional Photography by Tom Green,
Kelly J. Mihalcoe, and Lael White

New Photography Directed by
Carson O. Hudson, Jr.

Text by Suzanne E. Coffman

The Colonial Williamsburg Foundation
Williamsburg, Virginia

Library of Congress Cataloging-in-Publication Data

Doody, David M.
    Williamsburg—three hundred years : freedom's journey / photography by
David M. Doody ; additional photography by Tom Green, Kelly J. Mihalcoe,
and Lael White ; new photography directed by Carson O. Hudson, Jr. ; text
by Suzanne E. Coffman.
        p. cm.
    ISBN 0-87935-192-6 (pbk.)
    1. Williamsburg (Va.)—History Pictorial works. 2. Historical reenact-
ments—Virginia—Williamsburg. I. Coffman, Suzanne E., 1958– II. Title.
    F234.W7 D67 1999
    975.5'4252—dc21

                                                    99-28789
                                                    CIP

Designed by Helen Mageras

Printed in China

The images on pages 10–13 and on the left of page 19 are reproduced courtesy the
Jamestown–Yorktown Foundation, Williamsburg, Virginia. The photograph of Chief
William H. "Swift Eagle" Miles on page 17 is reproduced with the kind permission of
his son, Chief William P. Miles.

Previous page: Forty-three years after he helped America win its freedom from Great
Britain, the Marquis de Lafayette returned to the United States. Everywhere he went,
Americans greeted him as a hero. On October 20, 1824, such notable Virginians as
Governor James Pleasants and U. S. Chief Justice John Marshall attended a dinner
held in Lafayette's honor at Williamsburg's Raleigh Tavern.

PREFACE

*W*illiamsburg—*Three Hundred Years: Freedom's Journey* re-creates in photographs and words moments from the history of Williamsburg, Virginia. From 1699 to 1780, when Williamsburg was the capital of Virginia, the town's story was in many ways Virginia's story. What happened here affected people throughout the colony and later the commonwealth.

Williamsburg also had an impact on the other colonies and the nation. Events that occurred here and the people who participated in them helped form the values on which the United States was founded. During the Revolutionary era, Virginians meeting in Williamsburg helped lead the thirteen colonies to independence. Because the Revolution was one of the most important periods in the town's history, a large portion of this book is devoted to that time and to people's experiences during it.

For many Williamsburg citizens, however, what happened in town before 1765 and after 1781 was just as important. *Williamsburg—Three Hundred Years* also looks at these occurrences. Some, such as the Marquis de Lafayette's return in 1824 and the Civil War, were of national importance. Others had local significance. But all contributed to the development of the town and the lives of its citizens.

We hope that you will enjoy this introduction to Williamsburg's history and that *Williamsburg—Three Hundred Years* will whet your appetite to learn more about the city and its people.

PROLOGUE

*T*he land lay between two rivers that flowed to a bay. Pines and hardwoods grew in abundance. Game and fowl inhabited the forests, and the rivers teemed with fish. Although the climate was relatively mild, the winters were harsher than they are today.

The first immigrants probably came from Asia. They settled along the rivers, where they developed a distinct culture and way of life.

The men hunted in the forests and fished the rivers. The women cooked and preserved the meat and fish the men brought back to the village. They grew crops on the land and gathered berries and nuts in the woods. The immigrants cured animal hides for clothing.

BEFORE THERE WAS WILLIAMSBURG

*I*n spring 1607, a new group of immigrants arrived. Europeans had been trading and
interacting with the Native Americans for more
than a century, but these men were different:
they had come to stay.

The 104 Englishmen and boys had
crossed the Atlantic Ocean to search for wealth,
find a more accessible route to the riches of
the Orient, and convert the natives to Christianity. They called their destination *Virginia*.
The Virginia Company of London, a joint-
stock company chartered by King James I,
sponsored the venture.

The newcomers reached land on April 26,
1607. After exploring the region, they selected
a small peninsula as the location for their
settlement. On May 14, 1607, the colonists
landed and began unloading their supplies.
They named their new home *Jamestown* in
honor of the king. They christened the river
that flowed around the peninsula the *James*.

*D*espite the hardships of life in Virginia, settlers continued to come. The first women arrived in 1608. More soon followed.

The colony's survival still remained in doubt. Then John Rolfe tried growing West Indian tobacco in Virginia.

The first crop was shipped to England in 1614. European demand for this sweet tobacco ensured the colony's economic success and caused the colonists to devote more land to tobacco fields.

*T*obacco cultivation was labor-intensive. Although new immigrants continued to arrive from England, the colony experienced a labor shortage.

Around 1619, a Dutch ship brought a small group of Africans

to Virginia. The English were familiar with slavery, which existed throughout the world, but there was no slave system in the colony during this early period.

The settlers treated many of the newcomers—and many of the Africans brought to Virginia after them—as indentured servants. These Africans worked for white masters for several years, then received their freedom.

To make immigration to Virginia more attractive, the London Company stockholders decreed that the colony should have the kind of government found in English counties and towns. Deputy Governor George Yeardley called for elections.

On July 30, 1619, representatives called *burgesses* met with Yeardley and his Council in the church at Jamestown. The House of Burgesses was the first self-governing body in British North America. It served as the lower house of Virginia's legislature, the General Assembly. The Council acted as the upper house of the General Assembly.

The stunned survivors began to rebuild their lives, and an uneasy peace followed.

Because the London Company had mismanaged the colony, King James revoked the company's charter in 1624. Virginia became a royal colony.

Partly to defend against future Native American attacks, the settlers constructed a palisade across the peninsula between the James and York Rivers. Soon a community known as Middle Plantation grew up near the palisade.

𝒯he region's natives found themselves pushed off their lands as more colonists arrived and began growing tobacco. The natives' way of life was threatened.

On March 22, 1622, the Powhatans fought back with a brilliantly coordinated attack.

Nearly one-third of the English died in the uprising.

Although most of the colony was still a frontier, homes, churches, and cultivated fields began to dot the Tidewater.

Despite another native uprising in 1644 and two years of warfare that followed, Virginia continued to grow and prosper. Most colonists lived in impermanent wooden structures, but a few well-to-do Virginians built homes of brick.

*N*ot everyone shared in the wealth. As the seventeenth century progressed, landowners turned increasingly to people of African descent to satisfy their need for labor.

By the 1660s, most African-Virginians could not look forward to receiving freedom in exchange for years of toil. Instead, generations were born into slavery, and slavery became a key component of the colony's economic and social structure.

$\mathcal{S}$ome white men felt that they, too, had been left out of the picture. In April 1676, many former indentured servants joined Nathaniel Bacon in his attempt to wrest power from the landowners who controlled the colony.

Months of civil war followed, during which Bacon (a landowner himself and a member of the Council) and his followers burned the Statehouse at Jamestown. Bacon's death in October from the "Bloody Flux" (probably dysentery) ended the rebellion. The colony's government regained control of Virginia.

PRELUDE TO FREEDOM

The Statehouse burned again in October 1698. This time, Governor Francis Nicholson recommended that the capital be moved from Jamestown to Middle Plantation. On June 7, 1699, the General Assembly adopted *An Act directing the building the Capitoll and the City of Williamsburgh.*

Bruton Parish Church and the College of William and Mary were already located at Middle Plantation. Nicholson set about designing a city that incorporated these two landmarks and would, in the words of the act establishing the town, be "suitable for the accommodation and entertainment of a considerable number of persons, that of necessity must resort thither" to participate in the legislature and high courts.

Soon the once-quiet community was bustling with the activities of surveyors, carpenters, brickmakers, and undertakers (general contractors).

The relocated capital attracted new residents and numerous visitors. In 1712, English naturalist Mark Catesby joined his sister and brother-in-law in Williamsburg.

Catesby spent seven years studying the region's flora and fauna. After a second trip to the New World, he published a two-volume collection of his illustrations.

Other arrivals came under duress. Virginia's high courts convened in Williamsburg, and the Public Gaol often housed murderers, thieves, and other dangerous felons awaiting trial.

In January 1719, British naval officers brought fifteen pirates, members of the notorious Blackbeard's crew, to the Gaol. The miscreants had been captured in an expedition sponsored by Virginia's lieutenant governor, Alexander Spotswood. Blackbeard had died during the fierce battle.

On March 12, 1719, a court of admiralty met in the Capitol to try the pirates. Spotswood presided over the proceedings, which sentenced thirteen of the prisoners to death.

As the eighteenth century progressed, Williamsburg grew in size and importance. Brick public buildings symbolized the significance of the activities that occurred in town.

Much of the colony's business was conducted in the Capitol. Elected representatives enacted legislation in the House of Burgesses.

Virginia's highest courts, the General Court and the Court of Oyer and Terminer, met in the Capitol's other wing. In the Council Chamber above the General Courtroom, the governor and his Council discussed policy, approved legislation passed by the House, and received instructions from the Crown.

The imposing Governor's Palace underscored the governor's importance as the monarch's representative in Virginia. The lion and unicorn flanking the front gate reminded viewers that Virginia was a royal colony. A crown over the gate reinforced the idea that the colonists were the monarch's subjects. Weapons arrayed in the entrance hall symbolized the Crown's power.

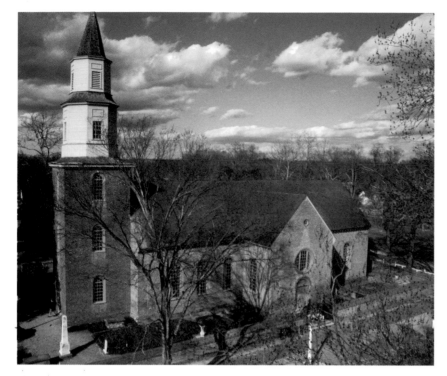

The College of William and Mary also expanded. In 1723, The Brafferton was constructed to house Native American students. Nine years later, a chapel was added to the main building. The President's House was erected in 1732–1733.

The Magazine housed weapons and ammunition to be used for the colony's protection.

Bruton Parish Church took on new importance as the church the royal governor attended. The councillors and burgesses also worshipped there when they were in town. The original church building could not accommodate all of the people who came to Williamsburg to do government business, and a larger structure was completed in 1715.

Williamsburg became the colony's leading economic, cultural, and social center. Residents worked year-round behind the scenes to keep the business of government running smoothly.

The number and kinds of artisans in town increased.

William Parks founded the colony's first newspaper in 1736. People throughout Virginia relied on the *Virginia Gazette* to keep informed. Parks also became the colony's first public printer.

Medical practitioners offered their services, and milliners, tailors, and wigmakers helped customers stay fashionable. Merchants competed for the custom of residents and people who came to town. Tavern keepers housed and fed out-of-towners.

Williamsburg's population swelled during the quarterly meetings of the high courts, or *Publick Times*. Attorneys and litigants arrived to participate in court cases, and merchants met with their peers. Burgesses added to the numbers if the General Assembly was in session.

Publick Times were the town's main social seasons. People danced at balls held in taverns and public buildings. Locals and visitors alike enjoyed the offerings at Williamsburg's playhouse, the first in British North America.

Traveling troupes performed for the crowds, which also attracted itinerant vendors. Enslaved residents heard news of absent family members and friends from blacks who accompanied their white masters to the capital.

𝓘n December 1739, evangelist George Whitefield gave Williamsburg a taste of the Great Awakening. His fiery oratory and message of personal salvation for all—regardless of class or race—contrasted with the liturgy usually heard in Bruton Parish Church.

The Great Awakening's emotional fervor and promise of a personal relationship with God appealed to the enslaved in a way that restrained, hierarchical Anglicanism could not. Many African-Virginians embraced evangelical Christianity.

𝒜frican-Americans appeared everywhere one looked in eighteenth-century Williamsburg. Their labor kept the town running.

Enslaved and free blacks developed a rich culture that blended African and European traditions. Storytelling taught children family history, values, religion, and how to get along with white people.

The jumpin' the broom ceremony united enslaved couples, although white laws did not recognize slave marriages. Music and dance enhanced the sense of community and helped ease the burdens of hard labor and separation from loved ones.

*V*irginia's capital became a proving ground for the colony's leaders. In October 1753, Lieutenant Governor Robert Dinwiddie commissioned twenty-one-year-old George Washington to deliver a message to the commander of French troops in the Ohio country. The message contained George II's protest against French encroachments on British territory.

Dinwiddie's emissary returned to Williamsburg in January 1754. People throughout the colony lauded Washington as a hero after the *Virginia Gazette* printed his report on his dangerous journey.

The French ignored the king's message, and war broke out later in 1754. Both the British and the French courted Native Americans as allies in the struggle. Washington served in the campaign against the French until the end of 1758 and often visited Williamsburg to report on military matters.

O n February 22, 1759, Washington took his seat in the House of Burgesses. His fourteen years in the House honed his skills as a political leader.

The following month, the new burgess returned to the capital with his bride, Martha Custis. After their marriage, Washington managed the Williamsburg property that Martha had inherited from her first husband.

Experiences in Williamsburg also shaped Thomas Jefferson. The Albemarle County resident first came to the capital around March 1760 to attend the College of William and Mary.

Because he was the cousin of Peyton and John Randolph, Jefferson gained immediate entrée to Williamsburg society. A talented amateur musician, he also found himself participating in the weekly concerts Lieutenant Governor Francis Fauquier held at the Governor's Palace.

In 1762, Jefferson began reading law under George Wythe. The young man had often enjoyed the noted jurist's hospitality.

Patrick Henry's association with Williamsburg began less auspiciously in April 1760, when he came to the capital to be examined for a law license. Henry's unspectacular performance caused one examiner—George Wythe—to refuse to sign the license. The three other examiners signed only reluctantly. Despite this shaky start, Henry soon began making a name for himself as an attorney in Goochland County.

*A*s the second half of the eighteenth century began, most Virginians thought of themselves as loyal subjects of the king. They believed that they possessed the same rights and privileges as their counterparts in England and that the king, his ministers, and Parliament had the colonists' best interests at heart.

This view was challenged in April 1765, when word reached the colony that Parliament had enacted the Stamp Act. Scheduled to go into effect in the fall, the act required a tax stamp on many colonial items, including newspapers, pamphlets, legal papers—even playing cards and dice. The moneys raised would be used for the colonies' defense.

Great Britain was in debt from several years of war in North America, Europe, and India. The British government also needed money to administer the vast North American territories it had gained two years earlier in its victory over France. English politicians maintained that the colonists should help pay these costs.

The Americans saw things differently. It was their right as Englishmen, they argued, to be taxed *only* by an elected body, such as each colony's legislature. The colonists elected no representatives to Parliament. Parliament therefore had no authority to tax them.

In Virginia's House of Burgesses, the Stamp Act sparked angry debate.

Freshman burgess Patrick Henry led the protest against the Stamp Act, introducing several resolutions against it on May 29, 1765. The following day, he made an impassioned speech in favor of his resolves.

Henry's statement that "Tarquin and Caesar had each his Brutus, Charles the First his Cromwell, and George the Third . . ." provoked cries of "Treason!" from the other legislators. Nevertheless, the House of Burgesses narrowly adopted the resolutions. The burgesses later deleted one of the resolves from the record as too radical.

*N*o one knew what would happen. On October 30, the colony's stamp agent, George Mercer, arrived in Williamsburg. An angry mob cornered him near the Capitol, and only the intervention of Lieutenant Governor Fauquier prevented a riot.

Mercer resigned the next day. No stamped paper was issued in Virginia, causing the *Virginia Gazette* and most public business to shut down when the Stamp Act went into effect on November 1.

*P*arliament repealed the Stamp Act in March 1766. Although most Virginians returned to politics as usual, some burgesses wanted an opposition press established in Williamsburg. At their invitation, printer William Rind moved to the capital from Annapolis, Maryland, in the spring.

*V*irginians' faith in the colony's leaders was shaken after John Robinson, the Speaker of the House of Burgesses and treasurer of the colony, died on May 11. Officials soon discovered that Robinson had loaned influential Virginians paper money slated for destruction. Cries of favoritism echoed throughout Virginia. At its next session, the House separated the Speaker's and the treasurer's offices.

*A*nother scandal erupted in June, after prominent Williamsburg resident John Chiswell killed a man in a Cumberland, Virginia, tavern. The local justices denied Chiswell bail and ordered that he be taken to the Public Gaol in Williamsburg to await trial in the high court.

As the sheriff and Chiswell rode into the capital, several Council members blocked the path with their carriage. The councillors forced the sheriff to release his prisoner on bail. Allegations of "gentry privilege" again raced through Virginia. Chiswell died unexpectedly in his Williamsburg home the day before his trial, and calm returned to the colony.

On May 17, the House adopted an address to King George III based on the burgesses' resolutions of the previous day. The governor, Norborne Berkeley, Baron de Botetourt, summoned the burgesses to the Council chamber and announced that he was dissolving the legislature.

The former burgesses immediately proceeded to the Raleigh Tavern. There they considered a proposal not to import British goods or to purchase items imported from Britain.

*P*olitical dissention surfaced again on May 16, 1769, when the House of Burgesses adopted resolutions protesting the Townshend Acts. The Townshend Acts taxed certain imports and also authorized the use of general search warrants in the colonies.

On May 18, eighty-eight of the men signed the
Nonimportation Agreement. Many of their constituents
later followed suit. In November 1769, Lord Botetourt
informed a new session of the legislature that the
Crown intended to repeal all of the duties imposed by
the Townshend Acts except that on tea.

*D*espite his response to the burgesses' Townshend Resolutions, Botetourt remained beloved. Virginians were grief-stricken when he died on October 15, 1770. A grand state funeral was held for the late governor, who was laid to rest in the crypt beneath the chapel at the College of William and Mary.

Botetourt's successor arrived in the capital on September 25, 1771. Like Botetourt, John Murray, fourth Earl of Dunmore, was a full governor rather than a lieutenant governor.

Although the political arena remained peaceful, the Crown's continued attempts to tax the colonies and gain more control over them worried some Virginians. On March 12, 1773, the House of Burgesses established a Committee of Correspondence to discuss these issues with the other colonial legislatures.

The following August, printer William Rind died. Rind had leaned toward the patriot cause but had printed opposing views as well.

The late printer left a wife, five children, and debts totaling more than £1,500. His widow, Clementina, sold off many of the family's belongings, took over publication of her late husband's *Virginia Gazette,* and, like him, was chosen public printer to the colony. She played an active role in the publication of her newspaper. Clementina Rind died a year after her husband.

*O*n February 26, 1774,
Williamsburg citizens rejoiced as
Charlotte, Lady Dunmore,
arrived with several of the
Dunmore children to take up
residence in the Governor's
Palace. Although tensions
existed between Britain and the
colonies—the Boston Tea Party
had occurred only two months
earlier—Virginians still considered themselves British subjects
and were excited to welcome the
royal governor's lady.

*D*evelopments in the spring,
however, shook Virginians'
confidence in the mother country. Around May 19, the colonists learned that the British
government intended to close
the port of Boston in retaliation
for the Tea Party. Virginians were
horrified. Closing the port would
cause great hardship for the
citizens of Boston.

   On May 24, the House of
Burgesses adopted a resolution
calling for Virginians to observe
a day of fasting, prayer, and
humiliation to show their
sympathy for Boston. When Lord
Dunmore read the resolution two
days later, he dissolved the
legislature. Nevertheless, that
evening the former burgesses
held a ball at the Capitol to
honor Lady Dunmore.

*J*une 1, 1774, found people throughout Virginia in church, praying for their brethren in Massachusetts. In Williamsburg, George Washington and many other burgesses led the townspeople in a solemn procession to Bruton Parish Church.

*O*n July 10, the governor left the capital to head a military expedition to the Ohio country. His goals were to avenge the deaths of settlers in the region and to strengthen Virginia's claim to the territory.

Dunmore may also have wanted to be out of the capital when the first Virginia Convention convened there in August. The colony's leaders had called the extra-legal Convention to consider Boston's proposal that the colonies cease all trade with Great Britain. The Convention adopted the measure and elected seven men to repre-sent Virginia at the Continen-tal Congress in Philadelphia.

$\mathcal{T}$ensions stayed high during the summer and fall. The British prime minister was burned in effigy throughout the colony.

On November 7, 1774, in an act reminiscent of the Boston Tea Party, men in Yorktown threw two half-chests of tea into the York River. The tea destroyed during the "Yorktown Tea Party" was intended for John Prentis and Company in Williamsburg.

Despite the political strife, Virginians were delighted when Lady Dunmore gave birth to a daughter in December and named her Virginia. A victorious Dunmore returned to the capital soon after Virginia's birth. On January 19, 1775, he hosted a ball at the Governor's Palace in honor of his daughter's christening and the queen's birthday.

The division between Virginia and the mother country widened the night of April 20–21, 1775, when Lord Dunmore ordered royal marines to confiscate the colony's gunpowder. The governor was acting on instructions from the Crown.

The marines were discovered in the act of taking the powder from the Magazine, and angry citizens gathered in Market Square. Only the persuasion of such moderate leaders as Speaker of the House of Burgesses Peyton Randolph and Williamsburg mayor John Dixon prevented the crowd from attacking the Palace.

As word of the theft spread, volunteers assembled in Fredericksburg, Virginia, to march on Williamsburg. Word that British soldiers—acting on the same orders from Britain as Dunmore—had fired on colonists at Lexington and Concord, Massachusetts, fueled the men's anger.

On April 29, however, the volunteers received messages from Peyton Randolph, George Washington, and two other congressional delegates asking them not to act. The men reluctantly disbanded.

An outraged Patrick Henry could not be mollified. On May 2, he convinced Hanover County patriots to endorse a march to Williamsburg, then left for the capital himself.

Henry and his 150 men set up camp about fifteen miles from Williamsburg. On May 4, Carter Braxton, the son-in-law of the colony's receiver general, brought Henry a note of exchange to pay for the stolen gunpowder. Henry refused the note but eventually accepted payment. He then dismissed his men and proceeded to Philadelphia to represent Virginia in the Continental Congress.

Early on June 8, 1775, Lord Dunmore and his family slipped out of the Palace. On June 24, several men broke into the abandoned residence, removed more than two hundred weapons from the entrance hall, and took them to the Magazine. Five days later, Lady Dunmore and the children sailed for England. Dunmore took up residence on a Royal Navy vessel.

When it became clear that the governor would not return to Williamsburg, the Virginia Convention created a Committee of Safety to govern the colony when the Convention was not in session. On August 21, 1775, the Convention established a professional army to replace the colony's volunteer companies.

*V*irginia's attorney general, John Randolph, became convinced that the colony would never reconcile with the mother country. In September 1775, he moved his family to England. Randolph's position as head of his household obligated his wife and unmarried daughters to accompany him.

His son refused to go. Despite his father's entreaties, Edmund Randolph stayed in the colonies and served in the Continental army as an aide to George Washington.

*J*ohn Randolph's older brother, Speaker of the House of Burgesses Peyton Randolph, also remained behind. By the summer of 1775, Peyton's transformation from moderate politician to patriot leader was complete. He served as president of the first and second Continental Congresses.

*R*evolutionary politics affected black as well as white Virginians as other loyalists moved their households to more remote parts of the colony, where they felt they would be safer, or out of Virginia entirely. Many slaves found themselves torn from family and friends when they were forced to relocate with their loyalist owners.

*I*n October 1775, Lord Dunmore began leading raids against the patriots. The Virginia Convention responded by sending a regiment to oppose him on October 26.

*O*n November 15, emboldened by his victories against the colonists, Dunmore issued a proclamation placing Virginia under martial law. He also offered freedom to any patriot-owned slave or indentured servant who would fight for the king. The news raced through the colony.

Dunmore's Emancipation Proclamation pushed conservative and moderate white Virginians into the patriot camp. The colonists believed that the governor was violating their property rights, because slaves legally were considered property. Virginians also feared that slaves who received weapons would attack their former owners.

The proclamation electrified the slave community. In lofts, outbuildings, and quarters throughout Virginia, slaves wondered: could they trust the British?

Some decided that the chance for freedom outweighed the risks. Others chose to stay near friends and relations.

*F*ighting continued in the colony. Some former slaves enlisted in Dunmore's Ethiopian Regiment and fought for the British

*B*y May 1776, most Virginians were convinced that Britain would never respect their rights. On May 6, forty-five burgesses assembled at the Capitol. There they declared the House of Burgesses dead.

   The former burgesses were also representatives to the fifth Virginia Convention. They joined the rest of the delegates as the Convention convened in the Capitol.

One of the most important issues the fifth Virginia Convention considered was whether or not to instruct Virginia's representatives in Philadelphia to propose independence for the thirteen colonies. On May 15, 1776, after intense debate, the Convention voted unanimously in favor of the Resolution for Independence.

Immediately after the vote, men replaced the British flag flying over the Capitol with the Grand Union flag of George Washington's army. Thomas Nelson set off for Philadelphia to deliver the resolution to Virginia's congressional delegation.

Williamsburg celebrated the Resolution for Independence with military parades and illuminations. Three weeks later, Virginian Richard Henry Lee stood before the Continental Congress and proposed that the "United Colonies" break away from England. His motion led to the writing and adoption of the Declaration of Independence—and the birth of the United States of America.

The Convention turned to the business of creating a government for the new state. The delegates adopted a Declaration of Rights on June 12 and a constitution on June 29. Newspapers quickly spread the word.

On July 6, Patrick Henry was sworn in as the Commonwealth of Virginia's first governor. Henry was seriously ill, possibly with malaria.

Some feared the governor would die before he could administer the oath of office to the state's other officials. Henry managed to accomplish that duty, then left the capital to recuperate at his home in Hanover County. Upon returning to Williamsburg, he took up residence in the Governor's Palace.

Word that Congress had adopted the Declaration of Independence—written in large part by Thomas Jefferson—reached Williamsburg in mid-July. Governor Henry issued a proclamation about the Declaration on July 25. That day, local attorney Benjamin Waller read Jefferson's stirring words to a crowd that had gathered at the Courthouse.

Jefferson remained active in Virginia politics. On June 1, 1779, he succeeded Patrick Henry as the commonwealth's chief executive. Governor Jefferson's wife and two young daughters moved with him to the Governor's Palace.

On June 16, 1779, a notorious prisoner arrived in the capital. Henry Hamilton, the lieutenant governor of Detroit, was called the "Hair-Buyer" because of rumors that he had paid Native American allies for American scalps. Governor Jefferson refused to see the prisoner, despite Hamilton's rank.

As the Revolutionary War dragged on, people became concerned that Williamsburg's location made the town vulnerable to British attack. Virginia had also grown geographically, and the capital was now far from the state's outlying regions. The legislature decided to move the capital to a more defensible and central site.

On April 7, 1780, the government relocated to Richmond. Armed guards accompanied the state's official records on the journey.

Many Williamsburg residents who relied on the state government for business decided to move to the new capital as well. Although Williamsburg remained the home of the College of William and Mary and the Public Hospital, the town was much quieter and less prosperous after the government left.

The war came to Williamsburg on June 25, 1781, when British General Cornwallis's troops marched into town. For a week and a half, British and Hessian troops occupied Williamsburg. Everywhere residents looked, they saw soldiers and camp followers.

Some enslaved African-Virginians took advantage of the British presence to run to freedom.

The British commandeered residences and supplies. They also brought two other hardships with them: swarms of nasty, biting flies, and smallpox. Because several of her slaves had left, Betty Randolph, the widow of Speaker Peyton Randolph, had little help as she cared for a relative stricken with the pox.

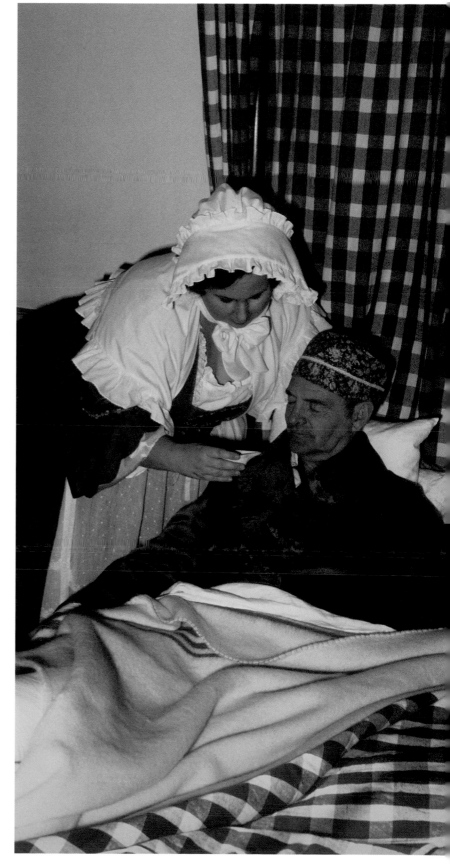

*C*ornwallis's forces left Williamsburg for Yorktown on July 4, 1781. American troops under the command of the Marquis de Lafayette soon replaced them.

Although residents were happy to
see Lafayette's troops, in some ways, the
American soldiers' presence felt like
another invasion.

George Washington and French General Rochambeau arrived on September 14. The two generals began planning the Yorktown Campaign.

The majority of American and French forces gathered in Williamsburg on September 26 and left for Yorktown two days later. On October 19, 1781, Cornwallis surrendered. Some sporadic fighting followed the surrender, but for all intents and purposes, the war was over.

French and American troops returned to Williamsburg, where the Governor's Palace served as a hospital for soldiers wounded at Yorktown. On December 22, 1781, the Palace caught fire. No one was injured, but the blaze destroyed the building.

Rochambeau remained in Williamsburg until July 1, 1782. By mid-August, the last French troops were gone.

The Revolutionary War ended officially on September 3, 1783, when U. S. and British negotiators signed the Treaty of Paris. Like Americans throughout the country, Williamsburg residents turned their attention from winning independence to preserving it.

TRIUMPHS AND TURMOIL

For a number of years, postwar Williamsburg enjoyed a quiet existence. The town relived some of its former glory October 20–22, 1824, when the Marquis de Lafayette visited during his triumphant tour of the United States.

Lafayette had known hard times since the War for Independence. The French government had imprisoned him during the French Revolution. Although he was released—partially because of the intervention of such allies as George Washington—the marquis never experienced the popularity in his own country that he had found in America during the Revolutionary War.

Throughout the United States, Americans who had lived through the Revolution and those born long after it greeted Lafayette as a hero. The people of Williamsburg were no exception. Everywhere the marquis went in town, crowds cheered him.

Colonel Burwell Bassett of Bassett Hall hosted a dinner for Lafayette in the Apollo Room of the Raleigh Tavern. A long list of notable Virginians, including the governor, the chief justice of the United States, and members of the state Council, joined them.

*D*uring the decades that followed Lafayette's visit, Williamsburg residents got caught up in the sectional strife developing between the Northern and Southern states. In October 1859, men of the town formed a volunteer company in response to news of John Brown's raid on the Federal arsenal at Harpers Ferry, Virginia (now West Virginia).

As North–South relations continued to deteriorate, most of Williamsburg's white residents sided firmly with the South. On May 23, 1861, Virginia seceded from the Union. Townspeople cheered as their neighbors raised secession flags.

GOD·AND·OUR·RIGHT

Residents enthusiastically supported the Southern war effort. Men enlisted. Women held fund-raisers, prepared rations, sponsored balls and entertainments for the Confederate soldiers mustering in the area, and opened their homes to the young volunteers.

Williamsburg's fortunes changed on May 5, 1862, when Union and Confederate soldiers clashed just outside town.

Residents listened to the cannon fire all day, then watched as Confederate wounded poured into town. Some people fled with the retreating Southern army.

The next morning, those who had stayed behind emerged from their homes into an occupied town. Cynthia Beverley Tucker Coleman glared with hatred at the Union soldier standing in front of her house, not realizing that Federal troops had been posted throughout Williamsburg to protect the residents.

Every public building had become a makeshift hospital. Wounded from both armies littered Market Square; the courtyard at the College of William and Mary; the churches, including Bruton Parish Church, Williamsburg Baptist Church, and the African Baptist Church; and people's lawns.

The townspeople went to work. Women prepared food and drink and helped nurse the injured. Local doctors treated the wounded of both sides.

People took ailing soldiers into their homes. Captain John Willis Lea of the Fifth North Carolina Infantry convalesced with the Durfey family at Bassett Hall. His injury had a happy resolution; three months after the Battle of Williamsburg, Lea and one of the Durfey daughters, Margaret, married. Lea's West Point classmate, Captain George Armstrong Custer of the Union army, stood as his best man.

𝓔nslaved residents had mixed reactions to the events. Some ran away to freedom. Others welcomed the Federal troops. Still others viewed the soldiers with suspicion. One woman was surprised that the Union troops did not have horns—contrary to her mistress's assertions.

As the occupation wore on, most of the white women in town found ways to show their distaste for the occupying forces. Williamsburg ladies often refused to walk on the same side of the street as the "Yankees." If no other option was available, they walked as far from the soldiers as possible, pulling their skirts aside to avoid touching the men.

Although Confederate raiders attacked Williamsburg in 1862, 1863, and 1865, the town remained under Federal control until the war ended in April 1865. The last Union soldiers left in September 1865.

*L*ike most Southerners, Williamsburg residents mourned the Confederacy. And like most of the South, the town experienced poverty after the Civil War. Eighteenth-century structures were crumbling, but most people had no money to repair—or raze—them.

In 1884, Cynthia Beverley Tucker Coleman founded the Catherine Memorial Society to mend the tombs and walls at Bruton Parish Church. Named for Mrs. Coleman's late daughter, the society was the first known restoration effort in Williamsburg.

The Catherine Memorial Society stimulated general interest in historic preservation. In 1889, Mrs. Coleman and Mary Jeffrey Galt organized the Association for the Preservation of Virginia Antiquities.

One of the first projects the new association undertook was saving the Magazine. Used as everything from a dancing school to a stable, the building had deteriorated badly. The association bought and stabilized the Magazine and eventually installed a colonial museum in it.

*W*hile the Association for the Preservation of Virginia Antiquities was rescuing colonial sites, progress was altering the Williamsburg landscape. By the early twentieth century, Williamsburg was a typical Southern town that boasted such modern conveniences as paved streets, electricity, and a movie theater. Remnants of the town's colonial past were hidden or nearly unrecognizable.

he Reverend W. A. R. Goodwin saw beneath the asphalt and around the power lines. Goodwin heard the echoes of George Washington, Thomas Jefferson, and Patrick Henry when he walked through town. He became convinced that Williamsburg should be restored to its Revolutionary-era appearance.

Goodwin searched for a benefactor to fund the research, restoration, and reconstruction his dream would require. After being rebuffed by some people and encountering only polite interest from others, he met Standard Oil heir John D. Rockefeller, Jr.

Rockefeller visited Williamsburg briefly in March 1926 and again on November 27, 1926. After viewing renovations at the George Wythe House and strolling with Goodwin through the woods at Bassett Hall, Rockefeller asked to walk through town alone.

That evening, the philanthropist announced that he would fund the restoration of Virginia's colonial capital. Colonial Williamsburg would stand as a monument to the origins of American democracy.

*R*e-creating an entire colonial town was a monumental task, one never before attempted. Rockefeller and Goodwin hired a broad range of people and established a corporation to manage the project.

Archaeologists and historians uncovered the secrets of the past. Architects guided the restoration of original eighteenth- and early nineteenth-century buildings. Construction crews rebuilt structures that had long since disappeared. Laborers moved anachronistic buildings to locations outside the Historic Area. Landscape architects designed gardens.

Old answers sometimes solved new problems. Finding bricks suitable for reconstructing eighteenth-century buildings presented a challenge, so Colonial Williamsburg set up a wood-burning kiln in 1930. A team of North Carolina brickmakers was hired to make bricks by hand. The molder, "Babe" Sowers, produced an astonishing four thousand bricks each day. Other brickmakers could mold only half that number.

By 1934, the Capitol, Governor's Palace, Raleigh Tavern, and ninety-one other buildings had been reconstructed, sixty-one original buildings restored, and several colonial gardens re-created. At the official opening of the Historic Area in October, President Franklin D. Roosevelt called Duke of Gloucester Street "the most historic avenue in America."

EPILOGUE

The rebirth of the colonial capital helped stimulate the growth of the Williamsburg area. Just as eighteenth-century Virginians had flocked to Williamsburg, twentieth-century Americans came to see the re-created colonial town. Hotels, restaurants, stores, and other attractions sprang up to serve Williamsburg's burgeoning tourist trade. Today, millions of people visit the area each year.

*W*hat was once the heart of Williamsburg is now a living history museum where visitors learn about Virginia's contribution to the Revolution. Over time, the way Colonial Williamsburg tells this story has evolved. The tale no longer focuses solely on the white, upper-class men who led the colony—and the country—to revolution, or on the politics of the era.

*V*isitors learn what *revolution* and *freedom* meant to African-Virginians and to women. Family life and childhood have been added to the picture. Programs feature the working poor as well as the gentry and address such universal topics as birth and death and sickness and health.

$\mathcal{H}$ow people visit Colonial Williamsburg has also expanded. Satellite technology enables school-children throughout the country to participate in electronic field trips broad-cast live to their schools. People worldwide log in on Colonial Williamsburg's web site to make virtual visits to the museum.

Colonial Williamsburg calls the history it teaches *Becoming Americans: Our Struggle to Be Both Free and Equal.* Becoming Americans tells the story of how diverse peoples with different and sometimes conflicting personal ambitions evolved into a society that values both liberty and equality and that struggles still to make these values a reality for all citizens.

The process of becoming Americans continues today. Every December, immigrants gather in the reconstructed Capitol to become U. S. citizens. On the site where generations of Virginians helped form the principles of American democracy, the immigrants pledge to "support and defend the Constitution and laws of the United States of America." The new Americans bring differing values, beliefs, and goals to citizenship, and the definitions of *American* and *freedom* continue to evolve.

ACKNOWLEDGMENTS

The following individuals are featured in the photographs in this book or provided invaluable assistance behind the scenes. To all we extend our thanks.

Bob Albergotti
Laura Arnette
Brian Ashlock
Tom Austin
Jay Ayscue
Susannah Badgett
Harvey Bakari
Willie Balderson
Bill Barker
Brooke Barrows
John Barrows
Andrew Barry
Stan Beadle
Sven Berg
Susan Berquist
Nathan Betz
Dan Bjick
Harold Blount
John Boag
Philip Bond
Terry T. Bond
Ted Boscano
Sandy Bradshaw
Antoinette Brennan
Lauren Brown
William A. Brown III
Tab Broyles
Frances Burroughs
Catherine Bush
Charles Bush
Kevin Bushee
John Caramia
Ronald Carnegie
Cary Carson
Clip Carson
Bob Chandler
Karen Clancy
Juleigh Clark
Michelle Clawson
Don Coleman
Daryle Combs
Edwin D. Cooke III
John Cooke
Dennis Cotner
Mark Couvillon
Danielle Crowell
James Curtis
Gina DeAngelis
Thomas DeRose
Irvin Diehl

Susan Dippre
Jim Dorsey
Kathy Dunn
Amy Edmondson
Rod Faulkner
Christoph Fehrenbach
Bill Ferguson
Jack Ferguson
Joe Ferguson
Kendra Fields
Kelly Fisk
Ryan Fletcher
Jack Flintom
Naomi Frazier
Richard Frazier
Diana Freedman
Jeremy Fried
Leia Gary
Jay Gaynor
Shayne Gilliam
Patrick Golden
Thomas Gore
Elizabeth Graft
John Greenman
Cathy Grosfils
Rita Grove
Rick Guthrie
John Hamant
John Hamrick
Jane Hanson
Allison Harcourt
Dan Hard
Baxter Hardinge
Frank Hardister
George Hassell
Tom Hay
Bradley Hayes
Patrick Held
Cathleene Hellier
Christopher Hendricks
John Hill
Richard Hill
James S. Holloway
Steve Holloway
John Holt
Mark Howell
Carly Hudson
Eric Hunter
James Ingram
Bridgette Jackson

Danielle James
Emily James
Greg James
Arthur Johnson
Gregory Johnson
Sandra Johnson
Todd Johnson
Jennifer Jones
Joseph Jones
Preston Jones
Stevie Kauffman
Betty Kelly
Charlie Kendrick
Nancy Kiel
Robin Kipps
Don Kline
Bob Krasche
Mary Elizabeth Landon
Chris Lanier
Russ Lawson
Jim Leach
Brandon Lee
Nokomis Lemons
Shanna Livingston
Jim Loba
Harriott Lomax
Michael Lord
John Lowe
Kevin Majiala
Jack Marahrens
Joyce Marahrens
Marianne Martin
Tres Matthews
Katherine Maxey
Carl McClellan
Jim McDonald
Ryan McQueen
Ed Mekley
Chief William H. Miles
Anne Marie Millar
Sam Miller
Gene Mitchell
Stephen Moore
Henry E. Moseley
Wayne Moss
Eric Myall
Carlton Newsome
Richard Nicoll
Mary Norment
John B. Ogden

Keisha Oliver
Willie Parker
Lance Pedigo
Dick Peeling
Makeda Perry
Valerie Perry
Lee Peters
Scott Petrakis
Noel Poirier
Bill Potter
Lou Powers
Dirk T. Prince
Dylan Pritchett
B. J. Pryor
Wayne Randolph
Jerrold Ray
Charles Red
Robin Reed
Reenactor companies
Julie Richter
Marcel Riddick
Katy Ridgway
Peter Roberts
Burlyn Rogers
Bill Rose
Brenda Rosseau
Linda Rowe
D. A. Saguto
Karen Schlicht
Gregory John Schneck
Mark Schneider
Fred Scholpp
Abigail Schumann
Amanda Schumann
Claire Schumann
Richard Searles
Susan Shames
Becky Shelton
Elaine Shirley
Felix Simmons
Janine Skerry
Emily Smith
Hope Smith
Tim Smith
Dale Smoot
Earl Soles
Mark Sowell
Tom Spear
Kristen Spivey
Megan Spivey

Sharon Spradlin-Barrett
Monica Spry
Peter Stinely
Tom Summers
Timothy Sutphin
Richard Sylvia
Kyle Systermann
Shaye Systermann
Sylvia Tabb-Lee
David Tarleton
Karon Taylor
Marilyn Taylor
Osborne Taylor, Jr.
Tiffany Taylor
Dakari Taylor-Watson
Barbara Temple
Ken Treese
Christine Trowbridge
Dale Trowbridge
Darin Tschopp
Darci Tucker
John Turner
Sonny Tyler
Gerald K. Underdown
Carolyn Vassos
Jerry Veneziano
Sharon Walls
Robb Warren
Ron Warren
Dennis Watson
Herbert Watson
Robert Watson, Jr.
Edward Way
Ann Marie Weissert
Bill Weldon
Michael Wells
Marilyn Wetton
Bill White
Clay White
Jason Whitehead
Karen Wicker
Kirlett Williams
Larry Williams
Jeanne Willoz-Egnor
Tanya Wilson
Mary Wiseman
John Wright
Garland Wood
Paul Zelesnikar